IMAGES OF ENGLAND

ATHERTON
AND TYLDESLEY

IMAGES OF ENGLAND

ATHERTON
AND TYLDESLEY

TONY ASHCROFT

The History Press

Frontispiece: Alfred Southworth of Howe Bridge, an employee of the LUT, welding tram lines on the Newbrook Road at Atherton, probably in the late 1920s. He died in around 1956, aged seventy.

First published in 2003 by Tempus Publishing

Reprinted in 2013 by
The History Press
The Mill, Brimscombe Port,
Stroud, Gloucestershire, GL5 2QG
www.thehistorypress.co.uk

British Library Cataloguing in Publication Data.
A catalogue record for this book is available from the British Library.

ISBN 978 0 7524 3048 5

Typesetting and origination by
Tempus Publishing Limited
Printed in Great Britain.

Contents

An aerial view of Atherton in the 1970s.

Introduction

The two townships of Atherton and Tyldesley, which are the subjects of this book, form part of the Metropolitan Borough of Wigan which came into existence on 1 April 1974, when fourteen former Lancashire local authorities were merged.

Although Atherton (also called Chowbent), which lies approximately twelve miles north-west of Manchester and two and a half miles north north-east of Leigh, was an ancient settlement, records of its early history are somewhat fragmentary. Like many towns and villages which have witnessed changes in the way their locality has been spelt, Atherton's name has included the following: Aderton (1212), Athurton (1254), Aserton (1265) and Athirton (1293). However, the first record of its present-day spelling dates from 1332. Although the exact meaning of its name may be open to dispute, it most probably derived from Old English and Saxon elements in the language with words 'adre' and 'tun' meaning watercourse and settlement, or, possibly from the alder trees which flourished in the neighbourhood.

Whilst the names of Atherton and Chowbent are considered synonymous, they were in fact two distinct locations. Early references suggest that it was the latter name which took precedence. Whilst the area known as Atherton was a former chapelry in the parish and union of Leigh in the West Derby hundred, it included the village of Chowbent, a district surrounding the parish church. However, by the late nineteenth century the name had fallen into disuse. Like the name Atherton, Chowbent had several variations in its spelling, including Chollebynt and Shollebent in the mid-fourteenth century, the name probably being derived from Chowe's Field, a reference to a local family of the area.

The early history of the township was bound up with that of the Atherton family, as the office of Sheriff was held by Robert de Atherton in the reign of King John. The manor, which descended from Henry de Atherton, in the thirteenth century, remained in the family until Richard Atherton, the last direct male descendant died in 1726. After this the manor and estate passed into the Powys family through marriage, whose head bore the title Baron Lilford.

During the Civil War, the townspeople were supporters of the Parliamentarians in their struggle against the Crown. Their allegiance was influenced by John Atherton, Lord of the Manor (d. 1656) who was a captain in the army and a Presbyterian appointed to the county shrievalty in 1655.

Like many areas of the country, Atherton's main activities before the industrial revolution were agriculture, domestic-handloom weaving and silk manufacture, as well as nail and bolt making and coal mining. Frequently Athertonians were referred to as 'sparrowbills' after a type of local nail. The latter industries continued in production until recent times, although with the opening of the first cotton mill in 1776, the days of domestic weavers and spinners were numbered. By the beginning of the twentieth century, industrialisation was complete with the main sources of employment being in cotton mills, collieries and iron works.

Coal mining development in particular owed a great deal to the Fletcher family who dominated both the industrial and civic life of Atherton from the late eighteenth century through the Victoria and Edwardian eras.

The Fletchers were an ancient family whose various branches were particularly successful in coal mining operations across Lancashire. John Fletcher began the sinking of two shafts under a lease granted to him and Thomas Guest by Robert Vernon Atherton Gwillym in 1776. After his son John – along with others – had sunk Howe Bridge Pit in 1850, five more collieries were in operation by the 1870s. By 1875 the paternalistic partnership of Fletcher Burrows and Company was created, which provided model housing, social clubs, pithead baths and heated coal screening areas as well as building a school and church at Howe Bridge. The last pit, Chanters Colliery, closed due to the exhaustion of reserves in 1966.

The development of local government in Atherton had tended to follow that of the towns in Lancashire of a similar size with the population increasing from 3,249 on 1801 to 16,211 in 1901. A local board was formed in 1863 which was then succeeded in 1897 by an Urban District Council.

Unfortunately many of the old industries have now disappeared, to be replaced by small industrial units and a growing service sector. A large number of commuters work outside the area travelling to Wigan, Bolton and Manchester. However, a strong sense of community still remains.

Tyldesley or Tyldesley cum Shackerley, like Atherton, was a township and parochial district of Leigh Union which formed part of the West Derby hundred in the south division of Lancashire. It lies about three miles north east of Leigh and approximately ten miles from both Manchester and Wigan. Once again over the years there have been variations, which have included Tildesleia (c. 1210), Tyldesleye (1301), Tilesle (1322) and Tildeslegh (1357), although today's spelling was in use as early as 1292. Its derivation possibly stems from the Old English for the woodland clearing of a man called Tilwald.

Shackerley was regarded as a separate hamlet about a quarter of a mile north of the main township. Whilst very little is known of its early history, there is evidence of Roman occupation with a Roman road from Wigan (Coccium) to Manchester (Mamucium) running through the area. In 1947, two urns containing about 600 coins minted between AD 259 and AD 273 were found near to the route of this ancient road.

The manor of Tyldesley, along with three other unnamed manors, were dependent on the chief manor of Warrington before the Norman Conquest, and at the creation of the Barony of Warrington it was included in that fee. The manor and demesne lands were in the possession of the Tyldesley family for hundreds of years. The celebrated royalist and member of the family Sir Thomas Tyldesley was killed at the Battle of Wigan Lane on 25 August 1651, after having been shot in the back. Although he had lived at Myerscough, he had been Keeper of the King's Forest at Tyldesley and had once owned Morley's Hall at Astley. He is buried in Leigh parish church, whilst his portrait hangs in the Council Chamber of Leigh Town Hall. It was his son Edward, who in 1672 sold the paternal state to the Astleys. It then passed on to Thomas Johnson of Bolton who retained it until 1823, before he passed the property to his nephew George Ormerod of Chorlton, the noted historian of the County of Cheshire. In the mid-1820s Ormerod had lived at Tyldesley House, where his second son George Wareing Ormerod was born in 1810. He then moved to Sedbury Park in Gloucester where he died in 1873.

Modern-style local government in Tyldesley began on 7 September 1863 when the town adopted the Local Government Act of 1858. The first Local Board was elected on 24 October of the same year. Like Atherton, the Tyldesley population increased between the periods 1801 and 1901. In 1801 the figure stood at 3,009, whilst a century later this had grown to 14,843. From that time the town grew steadily. In 1894 another important step took place under a further Local Government Act of that year when the first Urban District Council was formed. Public amenity provision began to expand with the local authority taking control of the gas undertaking in 1876, the opening of the public swimming baths in 1879, the sewage works in 1884 and Tyldesley Park in 1902.

Like many of its neighbours, Tyldesley's main industries once centred on coal and cotton. Industrial unrest occurred in 1823 after a strike and lockout at Messrs Jones, spinners. Workers who were intent on an increase in their wages were sacked. The employer then replaced them with new hands who were trained in spinning. Very soon the mills were working to full capacity with the new workers (known as 'knobsticks') being paid the old wages. As these workers left the factories they were assaulted by the old spinners, so the employers provided beds in the factories and hired armed guards to protect them. Eventually the trouble ceased as the old hands sought work elsewhere.

Today, with land reclamation and housing development, the landscape may have changed quite dramatically but the centre still retains the bustling atmosphere of a market town.

Since 1974, Atherton and Tyldesley have been part of a large unitary authority, Wigan Metropolitan Borough, which was formed following local government re-organisation.

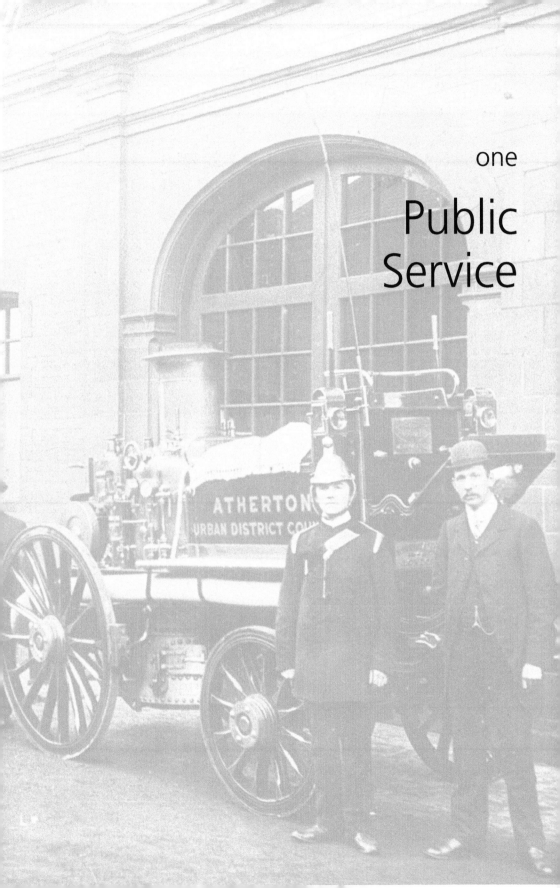

one

Public
Service

Above: In May 1938 the area had a royal visit from His Majesty King George VI and Queen Elizabeth. They arrived at Leigh railway station before travelling to Leigh Town Hall for various presentations. After their duties at Leigh, the King and Queen travelled along Market Street, Leigh Road and through Howe Bridge to Atherton on their way to Manchester. The photograph shows the royal convoy being greeted by 1,114 enthusiastic school children from Hesketh Fletcher, Howe Bridge, St George's infants and St George's junior schools who were standing on the pavement opposite Atherton cemetery.

Opposite above: Queen Victoria's Diamond Jubilee was proclaimed from the obelisk, Market Street, in Atherton on 22 June 1897 by Dr Sephton JP, CC (Chairman of the District Council). After the congratulatory address had been given to the listening crowd, it was then sent to Her Majesty the Queen. The obelisk, which had been erected by Robert Vernon Atherton in 1781 at a cost of £32 16s 6d, was rebuilt in 1867.

Opposite below: In March 1932, during his three-day tour of Lancashire, the Duke of York paid a visit to Atherton. His itinerary included a visit to Briarcroft Boys' Club, before travelling to Gibfield Colliery where he was shown around the new pit-head baths which had a capacity of 380. He also saw the first-aid station and screen room. Here he is seen leaving Gibfield Colliery in the company of Mr S. Ramsden. Supt. McHardy is saluting the Duke, whilst behind him are Mr C. Fletcher and Mr R. A. Burrows JP.

Above left: John Buckley of Primrose Street, Tyldesley, was an octogenarian bachelor, who was born in Shuttle Street in 1812. At the start of his working life he was employed as a scavenger in the mill belonging to Messrs Burke, working from 5.30 a.m. until 8.00 p.m. with only fifty-five minutes for lunch and no breakfast or tea breaks. His wage was only 1s 6d per week. Later he became a handloom weaver, before moving to Wales where he worked as a clogger with Mr Peter Eckersley. He then returned to Tyldesley where he retired from work. In 1840 he founded the Tyldesley Mechanics Institute with Mr W. Lomax and others. He was a noted Congregationalist and teetotaller. By his will he bequeathed the sum of £200 for the erection of a public drinking fountain in the square. A noted historian Mr Buckley published his *Chronological History of Tyldesley* in 1878. He died whilst on holiday in Douglas, on the Isle of Man, and his body was brought back to Tyldesley, where it was buried in the cemetery.

Above right: Robert Isherwood JP of Canonbury House, Tyldesley, died in January 1905. Born in Tyldesley in 1845, the son of a handloom weaver, he began his working life down the pit to earn his own living. In April 1867 he was one of the striking miners who were against the Lancashire coal company's new policy of increasing the weight of coal by 70 or 80lbs into new tubs, without remuneration. During this strike he acted as a local secretary, the district being part of Wigan, whose agent was William Pickard JP. By 1875 he had become the miners' agent for the newly-formed Leigh and District Miners' Association. Six years later in 1881 Isherwood was appointed treasurer of the Lancashire and Cheshire Miner's Federation and also held the office of Vice President of the Cases Committee of the Miners' Permanent Relief Society. Through his perseverance, a Miners' Hall was erected in 1893. Besides being a chairman of the District Council, in 1897/98 he had been one of the first magistrates for the Borough of Leigh. In May 1906 to commemorate his work for the miners, a monument was erected over his grave for the sum of £150.

Sir Fred and Lady Longworth prepare to cut their special golden wedding cake at the Greyhound Hotel, Leigh, to celebrate fifty years of marriage on 23 November 1966. Fred and Mary Smith 'tied the knot' at Moor Lane Methodist church, Bolton, as their local Methodist church in Shuttle Street, Tyldesley, was not registered for marriages. Born at Farnworth in 1890, Fred and the family moved to Tyldesley, where his schooling was completed at Upper George Street. Aged fourteen he left school to work in the local pits, later becoming President of the Tyldesley and Astley NUM. In 1946 he joined Lancashire County Council and by 1964 had become its Chairman. His love of education enabled him to become governor of five local schools and by 1963 the girls' county secondary school in Tyldesley was named after him. In 1966 he was knighted by the Queen Mother for recognition of his work in the political and public services. He died on 29 August 1973.

Ken Blackburn, President of Tyldesley Rotary Club is seen welcoming the District Governor Mr Eli Butterworth (front row, centre left) along with other top table guests to the Club's thirty-first annual charter anniversary in January 1978. The venue for the celebration was Tyldesley British Legion.

Above: Crowds gathered outside the Atherton Free Public Library to witness the opening ceremony being performed by Lord Lilford on 24 May 1905. Although an earlier lending library had been in operation since the mid eighteenth-century run by trustees of Chowbent chapel, the new library had come into existence after the 1855 Public Library Act and the 1871 amendments which had been accepted in 1897, the year of Queen Victoria's Jubilee. A gift of £4,000 towards the cost had been made by the Carnegie Trust. The architects for the building which had fittings for about 12,000 volumes were Bradshaw and Gass of Bolton, whilst Rathbone & Sons of Atherton did the brickwork. Gervace C. Brian, the first librarian, remained in the post until 1945.

Previous page: The horse ambulance carriage, which had been purchased by the local police with money raised by public subscription, was handed over to Atherton District Council in June 1902. Conditions laid down included the proviso that the council house the ambulance and horses free of charge. The vehicle which had been constructed by Messrs Wilson and Stockall of Bury was able to carry two injured persons in recumbent positions. It had detachable rubber-tyred wheels, was well lit and ventilated. As well as being fitted with two stretchers, there were seats available for a doctor and nurses. The ambulance is seen here stationed outside Atherton Town Hall.

Right: Early 1900s. Two members of the Atherton branch of St John's Ambulance Brigade at this time were William and Walter Ewing (seen here).

Below: St John's Ambulance Brigade nurses from Atherton sit in their uniforms for an official photograph, *c.*1924.

Tyldesley regular constables together with a group of special constables based at the police station in Stanley Street took time off from their law-enforcement duties to sit for a formal photograph in 1919. Police Inspector William Lander who came to Tyldesley in March 1919 after succeeding Inspector Clegg, died in May 1925. Also in the force were Walter Evans and Richard Hargreaves, who were the sergeants at this time. However the number of constables decreased from sixteen in 1913 to twelve in 1924. During the war 'the specials' or ancillary police force guarded railway and other bridges, assisted in traffic duty and kept watch for air raids.

Members of the Atherton police force in 1915 operated from the police station in Water Street. In 1913 two sergeants (Tipping Turner and Herbert Rowbotham) were in charge of a force of seventeen constables.

A quintet of Tyldesley road sweepers, *c.* 1930. Wearing flat caps, and with scarves round their necks, they are poised for action with their brooms at the ready.

John William Heaton of No. 9 Park View, Atherton, celebrated his eightieth birthday in November 1949. Although he had worked as a stoker at Atherton Gas Works for forty years, he also used to be a 'knocker up'. When cotton mills started the working day in the early hours of the morning, workers used to avail themselves of the services of a person such as Mr Heaton, who used to go round and wake them up by tapping on the bedroom windows with a large stick. For almost fifteen years he 'knocked up' thirty customers daily between 4.30 a.m. and 6.00 a.m., walking at least two miles in the process. The stick itself was a pole with umbrella ribs fastened to one end.

Above: Firemen from Atherton fire station made themselves available for this formal photograph as they stood beside their horse-drawn fire engine outside the premises in Water Street in the early 1900s. The building, which was located opposite the gas works, housed the fire engine and ambulance carriage station, mortuary and store rooms. It was opened in October 1905. The large pair of folding doors was fitted with Leggatt's double-action bars, which allowed them to be opened in seconds in case of an emergency. The architectural work had been carried out by Mr F.H. Grimshaw, AMICE, the council's surveyor. In the centre of the yard was a covered manure receptacle as well as urinals. Sergeant S. Manly who was in charge of the Atherton fire brigade on its formation in 1881, retired in 1936 after having attended almost 500 fires.

Right above: Armorial bearings of the Urban District Council of Atherton were granted by Letters Patent on 29 May 1951 and coincided with the Festival of Britain celebrations. On a golden shield, a diagonal band of red features a lion's paw and on either side is a black diamond. The crest consists of a helmet with mantling above, which features a sparrowhawk with raised wings standing upon a golden shuttle with its right claw resting on a black millrind.

The lion's paw and the sparrowhawk represent Atherton's history through association with the important local families. The sparrowhawk is taken from the arms of the Athertons of Atherton, the last male of the family being Robert Atherton who died around 1785. His daughter, Henrietta Maria married the 2nd Baron Lilford who thus acquired the Atherton estates. His family is represented by the lion's paw which is taken from the Lilford arms.

The other heraldic symbols in the arms and crest represent local industries, both traditional and modern. The black diamonds are the conventional signs in heraldry for coal mining, an industry which had been carried on in Atherton since Tudor times. The cotton industry is represented by the shuttle in the crest whilst the millrind is the symbol for engineering, some form of which had been carried on in Atherton for centuries. The Latin motto is interpreted as 'By Wisdom and by Prudence'.

ATHERTON

Right below: Tyldesley-with-Shakerley's heraldic design displays the arms and crest of the family of Tyldesley: silver, a red chevron between three hillocks (or molehills) in natural colours such as green. Crest: A gold pelican in its piety, i.e. feeding its young with blood drawn from its own breast – a symbol of the Eucharist. In the minutes of the council the objects in the shield are described as 'three hills, or bongs'. 'Bongs' is a colloquialism for 'banks', a reference to the physical configuration of the district, which is sometimes called 'Tyldesley Banks' or 'Bongs'. The device of the UDC is remarkable in that whilst it consists of the arms of the old local family it also has a bearing on the topography of the district.

Opposite below: Members of Tyldesley fire brigade standing beside their horse-drawn engine outside the depot in Elliott Street at the turn of the twentieth century. By 1901 Thomas Brobbins had assumed captainship, although in April 1892 he had tendered his resignation along with the rest of the force of ten men *en masse*, as they had not been given permission by a managing director to enter the grounds of C. Wright's Resolution Mill after a storeroom had caught fire. The damage cost an estimated £3,000.

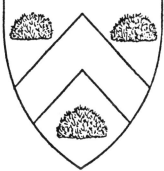

TYLDESLEY-WITH-SHAKERLEY

William Lomax, who lived at Meanley Street, Tyldesley, died on 3 May 1908 just a fortnight before his eighty-third birthday. Born at Lower Elliott Street, Tyldesley, in 1823 he began his working life as a handloom weaver before becoming a book keeper and then foreman in the mills of Burton & Sons, with whom he stayed until his retirement. Lomax was a dedicated educationalist and a founder member of the old Mechanics Institute as well as one of its trustees when the meetings were first established at Connicks Hole. He was also devoted to municipal work and served on the Local Board before becoming Chairman of the Local Authority and then, in 1905, Chairman of the first District Council. An ardent liberal, lifelong teetotaller and Anti-Corn League supporter he remained a bachelor.

two

At Home

Burton House and Burton cotton mills were established by James Burton who originated from Clitheroe. In his early years he became a managing partner in the firm of Chippendale & Co., Calico printers, before moving to Tyldesley in 1828. Here he became a partner with John and Richard Jennings Jones in the firm of Jones, Burton & Son. Messrs Jones however, were more interested in silk weaving and eventually moved to Bedford, Leigh, leaving Burton in sole control. By 1838 he was well established, as the firm of James Burton & Sons owned extensive properties in the town including seventy-four cottages and the King's Arms at the corner of Castle Street and Charles Street. Before his death in 1868 Barton had built Atherton Mill (1839) Lodge Mill (1853), Field Mill (1856) and Westfield (1860). His sons Oliver and Fred were his successors. During the 1920s the mills had been over capitalised and during the period of the great depression, the buildings were stripped of their machinery and finally demolished in 1926.

Above: Preston-born artist Arthur Devis, a pupil of Paul Tillemans, painted this picture in around 1746. It shows the owners of Atherton New Hall, Robert Gwillym and his family in a formal external setting, with their residence in the background.

Right: This engraving of Atherton Hall was first published in *Vitruvius Britannicus* (1725), the architect being William Wakefield (d.1730). Building work was begun by 'Mad' Richard Atherton in 1723 who intended the Hall to be the family's new seat. However, Richard died in 1726 and never saw the work, which was completed in 1742 at a cost of £63,000. In 1797 the Hall passed to the Lilford family by marriage. It remained empty for some time and because of prohibitive maintenance costs was demolished in 1825 by Richard Hodgkinson.

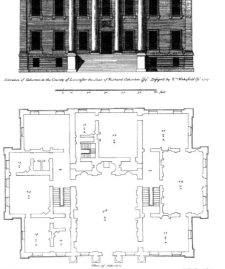

Above: Fulwell House in Tyldesley was probably built in the last decade of the eighteenth century by a Mr Gregory, manufacturer. By 1825 Thomas Kearsley had become owner of the property. Later occupants included John Jackson, James Bagley (who died there in April 1862) then his widow Ann. Charles Eckersley JP – who acquired the property at the beginning of the 1870s – lived there until his death in November 1919. In the early 1920s his son William offered the property as a gift to Tyldesley Council but this was refused by the narrowest of majorities. The house remained unoccupied until George Clapperton became tenant, but by 1935 it had been demolished. Evidently the house was quite a substantial one as the size of the grounds totalled 2.5 acres.

Opposite above: The Promenade, Leigh Road at Howe Bridge is so named because of its elevated pavement access to house numbers 191-147. The properties along this stretch are larger than those behind them and probably would have been occupied by firemen, overseers and miners assuming some vestige of responsibility. They were built by the benevolent mine owners Fletcher Burrows in 1873 for their workforce, the architect reputedly being the Dutchman Medland Taylor. In the middle of this row of properties is a former bathhouse, now a private house.

Opposite below: Gib(b) Fold in the early 1900s. At the time it had been used as a parsonage for Chowbent chapel and it was here that 'General' James Wood (minister of the chapel) died on 13 March 1759, in his eighty-seventh year. When a rebellion broke out in 1714, James Wood raised a considerable number of men from the congregation, trained them and then led them to Preston where they were employed in guarding the ford at Penwortham and bridges at Walton. Two of the people in the photograph are most probably Samuel Blakemore, nut and bolt manufacturer of Atherton and his wife Elizabeth who resided here. The building was demolished in 1958 to make way for a housing development.

Above: The Jig Brow area of Tyldesley consisted of these terraced houses. Taken in the early 1970s prior to their demolition, the scene is suggestive of a typical northern mill town with its cobbled roads and uneven pavements which are situated on an incline.

Right: By the late twentieth century, with improvements in sanitary conditions, outside toilets were generally a thing of the past. However in November 1990, this outside toilet attached to a property in Darlington Street East was still to be seen.

Opposite below: Mrs Burrows of Atherton relaxing in her living room, which has a typical 1950s feel. Her husband John was a bus driver and keen amateur photographer with the local photographic societies.

Above: A 1902 postcard showing Leigh Union workhouse offices and the receiving home. In accordance with the Poor Law Amendment Act, the Leigh Poor Law Union was created on 16 January 1837. The Union catered for a local population of about 26,000 and comprised the townships of Pennington, Westleigh, Bedford, Atherton, Astley, Tyldesley, Lowton and Culcheth. An earlier workhouse was situated in King Street, Leigh, but a new Union workhouse known as Atherleigh was built in Atherton in 1855. Originally the building was made up of two sections, each three storeys high and containing about fifty 'inmates' each. By July 1884 a new general hospital was added to the structure. The building continued to be used as a workhouse until 1945 when it became Atherleigh Hospital. By the early 1990s the hospital buildings were demolished to make way for a housing development.

Top: Cleworth Hall, an original half-timbered house built in the fourteenth century was destroyed in 1805 and replaced by a brick built-structure which has now disappeared. In 1594 the children of Anne and Nicholas Starkie, John aged ten and Anne age nine, found themselves at the centre of a case of 'demoniacal possession' which took place at the Hall. They were subject to fits and became 'speechless, senseless and as dead, and when they had use of their feet their tongues were taken from them, and all the time, they wist not what they did'. A well-known conjurer Edmund Hartley was asked to cure the children, which he apparently did. However, Starkie refused his demand for money and a horse in payment, so Hartley threatened trouble. On the same day seven people became 'possessed' of evil spirits. Exorcisms were carried out by two clergymen, Hartley was arrested and taken to Lancaster where he was convicted of witchcraft and hung. It later became a farmhouse which was demolished in the mid-twentieth century to make way for a housing development.

Above: Alder House, now a grade-II Listed building, is a three-storey stone mansion with mullioned windows and dates from 1697 when it was built for Ralph and Ann Astley. Ralph was a well-to-do iron merchant who was engaged in the local nail-making trade. In 1727 tradition has it that Ralph and Ann died within a day of each other, both being struck by lightning at the same time. By 1916 Fletcher Burrows had paid £1,750 for the house and its property in order to secure the mining rights. In 1922 Alder House was finally donated to Atherton Council, the premises being used as a maternity clinic. After local government re-organisation in 1974 it passed into the hands of Wigan Council. The property was put on the market in the late 1980s as there wasn't enough money for the building's restoration. A buyer was found but after a period of occupation, the premises in 2003 were once again up for sale.

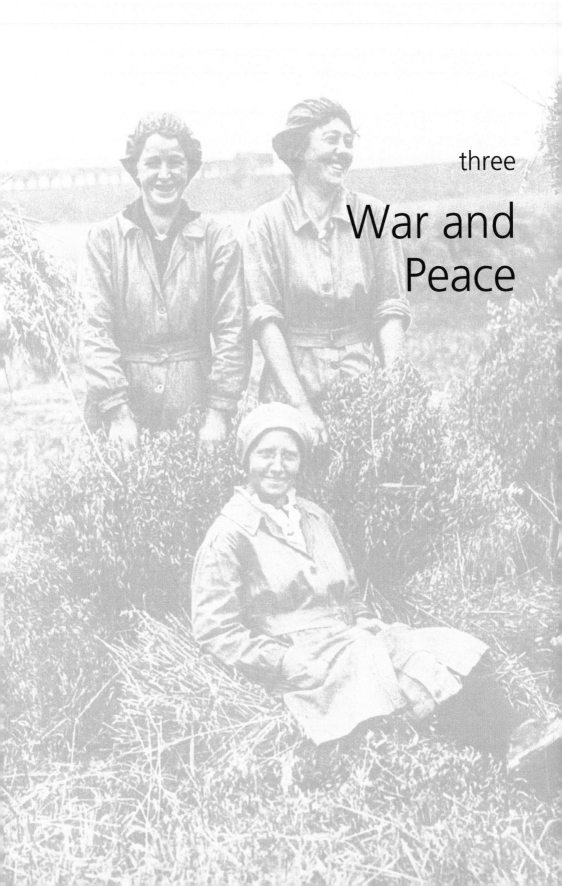

three

War and
Peace

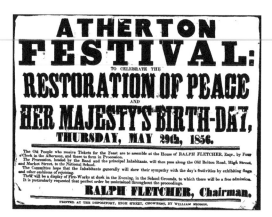

ATHERTON FESTIVAL:
TO CELEBRATE THE
RESTORATION OF PEACE
AND
HER MAJESTY'S BIRTH-DAY,
THURSDAY, MAY 29th, 1856.

The Old People who receive Tickets for the Feast are to assemble at the House of RALPH FLETCHER, Esqr., by Four o'Clock in the Afternoon, and there to form in Procession.
The Procession, headed by the Band and the principal Inhabitants, will then pass along the Old Bolton Road, High Street, and Market Street, to the National School.
The Committee hope that the Inhabitants generally will shew their sympathy with the day's festivities by exhibiting flags and other emblems of rejoicing.
There will be a display of Fire-Works at dusk in the Evening, in the School Grounds, to which there will be a free admission.
It is particularly requested that perfect order be maintained throughout the proceedings.

RALPH FLETCHER, Chairman.

PRINTED AT THE DEPOSITORY, HIGH STREET, CHOWBENT, BY WILLIAM MOSON.

Left: On 29 May 1856 local celebrations took place to commemorate the return of the great national restoration of peace after the Crimean War had ended in February of that year. The appointed day was also Queen Victoria's birthday, as well as being the anniversary of the restoration of Charles II to the throne. Employers of the district treated a workforce of over 600 to a dinner of roast beef at the Bear's Paw and King's Head inns, whilst twenty people over seventy years of age attended a small party on the lawn of Laburnum House – Ralph Fletcher's residence.

Above: In April 1912, there was a strike of miners employed in the Lancashire coalfield. Disturbances frequently broke out between the men on strike and those who were drafted in from outside the district to carry on working. As matters soon began to assume a graver aspect, troops were sent in to keep law and order. Amongst the 1,300 soldiers in the neighbourhood for this purpose was a regiment of 16th Lancers, who were normally based in Norwich. This group from the Lancers could be seen at Howebridge.

Opposite above: The Woodlands at Atherton, which was the residence of Mr M.F. Burrows JP, was converted into a hospital under the Atherton Division of the St John's Ambulance Brigade. The accommodation for the wounded men included five bedrooms; the large hall was used as a smoke room and a drawing room for reading, writing and recreation. Amongst the eight wounded and two sick soldiers who arrived on 18 November 1914 were: Private Latham, 2nd South Staffordshire Regiment, Bloxwich; Lance Corporal McNeir, 1st East Kents, Dover; Private Lennon, 3rd South Staffordshire Regiment, Birmingham; Private Onions, 1st South Staffordshire; Private Worthington, 2nd KOYLI, Long Eaton; Private Richardson, 2nd Bedfordshire, Bedford; Private Powers, 2nd Royal Iniskillin Dragoons, Waterford; Private Simpson, 2nd Sherwood Forester, Nottingham; Private Brown, 1st Cameron Highlanders, Blackwood (Scotland); Private Regan, 2nd Essex, East Ham, London.

In 1917 the Women's Land Army was formed by Mr Roland Prothero, then the Minister of Agriculture. Popularly known as 'The Forgotten Army' it comprised of girls from every walk of life. Here we see five such girls, appropriately dressed, as they take a few minutes off from their harvesting duties to smile for the camera. They were probably working on farmland in the Chanters area of Atherton.

Above: To celebrate the signing of the Peace Treaty following the end of the hostilities of the First World War, elderly residents of Atherton aged sixty or over, were treated to an old folks' tea towards the end of August 1919. More than 500 tickets were issued for the occasion. Formby Hall was the venue where two sittings had to take place, one at four o'clock and another an hour later. Besides the catering staff, thirty-two waitresses were employed to serve the meals. The Tramways Company allowed free rides to those attending the treat. After the meal, each guest was presented with either a packet of tea or 2oz tobacco, courtesy of Lord Lilford.

Above: The first officials of Atherton's Discharged and Demobilised Sailors and Soldiers club (DDSS) appeared together for this formal photograph in September 1919.

Right: On 6 May 1935, celebrations took place throughout the country to commemorate the Silver Jubilee of King George V. Amongst the local festivities was the floodlighting of the war memorial in Tyldesley cemetery. Although the cenotaph had been unveiled in November 1922 by Lord Crawford, it was decided that it needed renovating for this special occasion.

Opposite below: Although the Atherton DDSS had been established in October 1918 to offer help to those in need, whether members or non-members, it took nearly twelve months to secure permanent premises. A large detached house was acquired at the junction of High Street and Tyldesley Road, once the residence of Dr Marsh. The cost of purchase was £750 whilst a further £1,000 (raised by public subscription) was spent on renovation to make it a comfortable club. The club was officially opened by Mr M.F. Burrows JP in the presence of Mr I. Ormisher (President of the association) and others. At the time of opening, membership totalled about 400. The club finally wound up in October 2001.

The Local Defence Volunteers, formed in May 1940, were renamed the Home Guard at the end of July 1940. In September of that year Manchester Collieries Ltd boasted 1,800 members in this volunteer force. Here they can be seen in Gin Pits, Tyldesley, with St George's Pit in the background during their march past Manchester Colliery and Home Guard officials. However not all men at this early stage had uniforms.

Amongst the repatriated prisoners from Germany in October 1943 was Tyldesley resident L/Cpl James Eckersley of Park Street. He was captured in France during August 1940 whilst serving with the Welsh Guard, having joined them in 1928. He also saw service in Egypt.

One of the many military weddings that took place during the war years was that of Battery Quartermaster-Sergeant Ernest Williams and Nancy Isherwood. They tied the knot in August 1941 at Tyldesley chapel. The Revd R.J. Wallace officiated, whilst the organ was played by Mr Hampson. The bride wore a pink woollen suit with a hat to match also had a spray of stocks and scabias. The bridesmaids were Mrs Ann Isherwood (sister) and Miss Mary Williams (groom's sister), whilst the best man was AC/IHM Battersby.

Members of the Tyldesley branch of the Women's Junior Air Corps on parade, possibly in May 1943. They were taking part in Tyldesley's 'Salute the Soldiers' Week in an effort to raise money to transport a division from Tyldesley to Berlin. Here, a detachment of the corps prepares to look right as they approach the saluting base in Market Square.

21 March 1942 saw the beginning of Leigh, Tyldesley and Atherton's 'Warship Week' whose target was to raise £500,000 for HMS *Ulysses*. Each of the three districts had their own parade. Amongst the group of marchers was this WVS contingent from Tyldesley who marched from Mosley Common recreation ground to Shakerley Common. The salute was taken by Wing Commander Hamilton DSO, from the saluting base on the square at Tyldesley. The week was officially opened by Alderman Wright Robinson JP (Mayor of Manchester).

On 1 October 1944 over 200 competitors took part in the twenty-fifth County of Lancaster (Leigh) Battalion Home Guard weapons competition at Atherton. The range on which the competition took place had been constructed by men of 'A' Company on an abandoned pithead. The winning team was 'E' Company from Tyldesley.

A contingent of the Atherton Squadron ATC is seen here in September 1963.

four

Transport

Above: A group of workers employed by Prestwich Parker, bolt manufacturers of Atherton, prepare for a day trip in the late 1930s or early 1940s. Meeting outside the Albion Inn on Bag Lane, they were eagerly looking forward to a leisurely ride by a coach and four to Warburton Bridge, which spanned the Manchester Ship Canal in Cheshire.

Opposite above: Ordnance Survey six-inch map of Atherton and Tyldesley, 1894. The growth of the townships since 1849 can be measured by the introduction of rail links, and the increase in housing for the expanding population employed in the textile and mining industries.

Opposite below: Bolton Road service station, Atherton, ('Tel. Atherton 519') which opened for business in June 1962, was built on the site of a demolished cotton mill. Mr Rowland Meredith of New Brook Road was the first manager. Regent petrol was supplied to motorists who could fill up between the hours of 7 a.m. and 10 p.m. daily – vehicle servicing was also carried out on the premises.

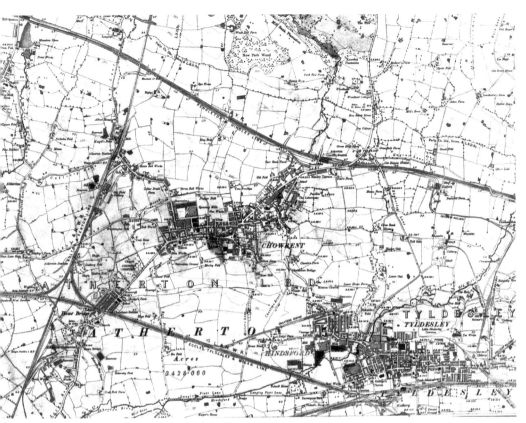

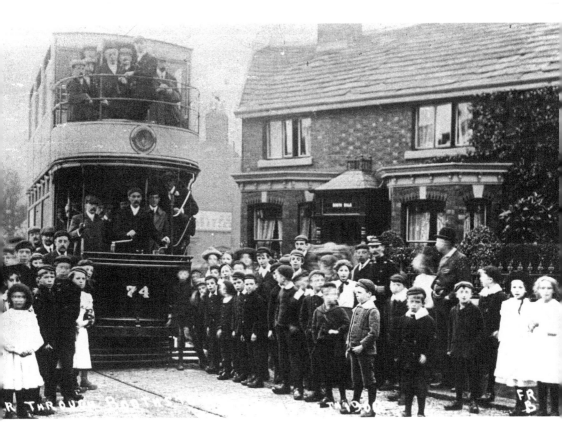

Above: On 17 September 1906, a crowd of onlookers came to see the first tramcar leave Boothstown for Swinton. This was a trial trip before the Board of Trades inspection took place the following week, after which the route was opened to the public.

Opposite above: Members of the Atherton Soldiers and Sailors Club eagerly await their charabanc trip in the early 1930s.

Opposite below: In 1901, workmen who were laying the tram lines in Shuttle Street, Tyldesley, had to contend with this group of onlookers.

Tyldesley station was opened on 24 August 1864 after the construction of a new railway line to run from Eccles to Tyldesley and Wigan, with a loop or branch line through Leigh to Bradshaw-leach. A general holiday was observed to celebrate the event. Sunday-school children and their teacher awaited the arrival of the opening train at one o'clock, in a field belonging to Mr Stott. The new line had been laid out by the engineer William Baker, whilst the contractor was a Mr W. Tredwell. The opening train travelled to Wigan where visitors from Preston joined it before returning to Tyldesley. On arrival directors and guests marched in procession to the new mill of E. and F. Burton where they were treated to a generous bill of fayre. The procession was headed by the band of 60th Rifles, followed by over 2,000 Sunday-school children as well as over 700 friendly society members, Worsley Yeomanry Band, the Tyldesley Church School, Drummond Fife Band and the Mossley Band. The cost of the line was approximately £15,000 per mile. The station closed in May 1969.

Above: In June 1963, railway enthusiasts were out in force to record the last railway engine to run on the Bag Lane-Pennington line before its closure.

Opposite: Fourteen-year-old Eric Boardman of Elliott Street in his LNWR uniform which he wore in 1912 when a railway employee.

Above: Passengers in 1923 wait patiently to board a double-decker bus belonging to the South Lancashire Transport Company.

Right: An electric milk float, with vehicle registration number GTJ 460 was supplied to a Lancashire dairy by the Lancaster Electrical Co. Specifications for this particular model included semi-enclosed side panels and a solid rear end. This vehicle was operated by Baxter's of Green Street, Tyldesley, around 1950. In a local telephone directory of the same period, an entry for Fred Baxter – who had the same address and telephone number – indicates that an ice-manufacturing business was also ran from the premises.

Opposite above: In the early 1900s, residents of Tyldesley and Boothstown were probably quite familiar with the figure of Peter Edge who travelled around the district with his mobile drapery business.

Opposite below: The milk must get through! After a heavy snow fall in 1939, employees of the Atherton and Hindsford branch of the Leigh Co-operative Society decide to use a horse-drawn sledge to keep supplies moving.

Employees of South Lancashire Transport using their overhead repair wagon to work on trolleybus wires in the 1950s.

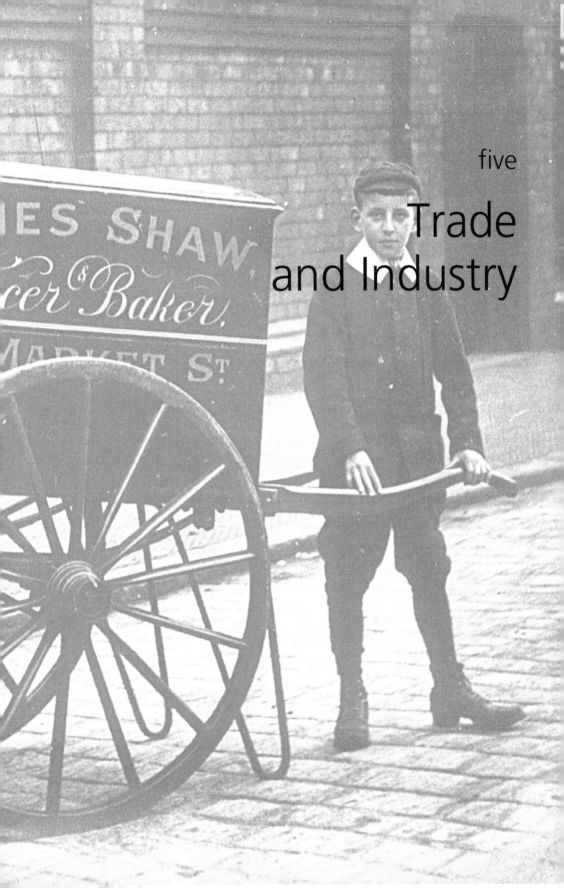

five

Trade
and Industry

Tyldesley girl Lois Heath, aged seventeen, was a card tenter at Laburnum Mills, Atherton. Lois was crowned Cotton Queen of Britain at the Tower Circus, Blackpool, in June 1931. Representing the Leigh area, Lois succeeded Miss Frances Lockett of Hyde. Wearing her regalia, she visited the Laburnum Mill in her official capacity as queen. In August of the same year she opened the £20,000 ornamental bridge over the marine lake at Southport. She married grenadier guardsman George Hartley of Warrington in February 1940. Lois died in February 1994 at the age of seventy-nine and is buried in Atherton cemetery.

A ring spinner at work in Caleb Wright's Barnfield Mill at Tyldesley in the 1980s.

Right: In the 1910s, local photographer Harry Parr of Underwood Terrace, Tyldesley, took his camera into a local mill to photograph this group of barefooted male cotton workers.

Below: In 1965, Combined English Mills (Spinners) Ltd, whose head office was at Atherton, were responsible for mills on fourteen different sites. These technicians were employed at No.6 mill in the contract testing department.

Previous pages: This mid-twentieth century aerial view of the Shuttle Street area of Tyldesley illustrates the extent of Caleb Wrights Banfield mills. Rebuilt in 1894 on the site of an earlier mill which had been destroyed by fire, it was demolished in the early 1990s to make way for a housing estate.

Above: Viyella House, *c.* 1940. This building situated on Gloucester Street, Atherton, was used as office accommodation for Howe Bridge Mills.

Left: A bobbin packer employed by Howe Bridge Spinning Company, at work in the mill around 1918.

Right: This image of Selina Cox, a scavenger employed by Howe Bridge Spinning Company in the No.2 spinning room, was probably taken in the late 1910s. A scavenger was a person who removed empty bobbins – usually the task of a juvenile who had not yet acquired the status of piecer.

Below: Edward Ormerod (1834-1894), colliery engineer, seen here in around 1890 standing in the centre of the picture, appears to be lecturing two of his workmen on the design of his different sized, safety winding detaching hooks. The design – which was first patented in 1868 and was originally known as the 'butterfly' – was a hook which attached to mine winding ropes just above the cage. If a cage over wound, the hook passed through a steel bell which was permanently installed on the shaft, clipped into the bell, detaching itself from the winding ropes, to hold the cage securely suspended. By 1954, over 10,000 safety devices had been produced, saving the lives of miners both in this and foreign countries.

The burial plot of Edward Ormerod in Atherton cemetery consists of a main headstone, together with a footstone which records the life-saving qualities of his successful 'butterfly' patent.

On 15 September 1913 the first colliery baths in the country were opened for miners at Gibfield Colliery. With a capacity of 400, it made use of the continental practice of using numbered clothes hangers, which enabled wet work clothes to be dried overnight. Here, a miner coming off his shift prepares to use the facilities.

Above: Pit brow girls were commonly employed as colliery surface workers, after they had been banned from working underground following the introduction of the 1842 Coal Mines Act. Most collieries had a regiment of female workers, with each pit having their own identifiable work dress. In this case, the women were employed in the screen room at Chanters Pit and their main duty was to pick out the coal, probably in the early 1900s.

Right: In June 1947, Michael James Carr of Ash Street, Tyldesley, was awarded the British Empire Medal (Civil Division) in the Birthday Honours List, in recognition of his services to the coal industry. Mr Carr retired in January 1947 after fifty-three years as a miner. He first entered the industry working three-and-a-half days a week for 1s 2d per day. For thirty-six years he worked at Astley Green, where he helped to sink the pits. During his career he advocated nationalisation and an eight-hour working day for miners.

Above: In May 1884 this group of workers employed by Johnson and Davies at their Excelsior works, Bolton Old Road, Atherton, appeared for a formal photograph. Excelsior, along with the Perseverance and Britannia works which were nearby, produced screws and bolts.

Left: One of the traditional industries of Atherton was that of nail making. This original document of 2 July 1741 is an inventory of the goods belonging to a Robert Smith who was a nailor by trade.

Opposite above: A worker on the production line in Prestwich Parker's nut and bolt factory, *c.* 1980. In 1869, Atherton could boast eleven nut and bolt manufacturers, but as time went on these numbers were reduced. Two of the early firms were those of James Prestwich and Robert Parker which eventually amalgamated in 1945 to form a company known as Prestwich Parker Ltd. By 1980, with a downturn in trade, the workforce was reduced by a third.

PARK SEATS 6FT LONG
GALVANIZED IRONWORK & TEAK TIMBER

We can
supply any
Type of
SEAT

Collapsible
Chairs

Tree Guards

W. I. Railings
etc.

Makers GORTON & BLAKEMORE LD.
ATHERTON FORGE   ATHERTON.
TEL. 55.

Above: In the 1950s, Atherton engineering firm Gorton and Blakemore Ltd constructed and erected buildings such as pit-head baths and garages. They were also makers of all kinds of steelwork, including steel-framed hay barns, railings and gates, collapsible garden chairs, bus shelters and park seats.

Above: 1915. The Tyldesley firm of John Grundy Ltd were heating engineers and general iron founders. The founder of the firm, John Grundy Senior, invented a form of heating apparatus which was installed in the local chapel in the late 1860s. His son John then took over the firm and made several improvements, later patenting the invention. By the 1880s, with the success of the heating system, the firm received commissions to install similar ones in both Truro and Derry Cathedrals.

Left: Staveley Ltd, an Atherton-based constructional engineering firm was first established in 1931. One early business contract in 1938 was for the building of this corrugated cinema at the Transfyndd army camp, Wales. By 1876 the firm had diversified its operation by becoming one of the first manufacturing companies outside the United States to specialise in the production of oil rig equipment.

The Queen's Award for Export Achievement was presented to the construction engineering company of William Hare at the firm's Astley works, Gin Pit Village in September 1978. The firm – founded in 1945– fabricated structural steelwork for the gas, oil and petrochemical industries. The Lord Lieutenant of Greater Manchester, Sir William Downward, presented the award to Mr Bartle Hodgkins, Chairman of Hare's. Also in the picture are Councillor Adam Hibbert (Mayor of Bolton) and Councillor Len Sumner (Mayor of Wigan).

Above: Taken in the late 1980s, this group of workers were celebrating their last day of work at Ward & Goldstone's factory at Atherton.

Overleaf: A Tyldesley grocery store in Morris Street, *c.* 1902. The young shopworker on the left is John William Yates. A fine selection of tinned goods and fresh meat is on display.

Above: In the 1930s Sally Caldwell owned this milliner's shop in Elliott Street, Tyldesley. Her window display gives a good idea of the fashions of the period.

Opposite: Sam Mather (1867-1959) standing in the doorway of 'Higham's Shop' at 265 Leigh Road, Howe Bridge, sometime during the 1930s. Mary 'Lizzie' Higham used to sell all manner of things in a poky front room. Shoes and clogs were also repaired by her brother. Sam Mather who lived a few doors away could still do 'the collier crouch' in his old age. Known locally as 'Sam Pam Nicky Nam' he played cornet in both the Atherton Temperance band and the Atherton public band which preceded it. He always wore a cap so that you never saw his head.

Right: In the period before the First World War, James Shaw managed a grocery business in Market Street, Atherton. One method of ensuring that the local deliveries of groceries and bread were made was by use of a hand cart. Here a couple of delivery boys, presumably employed by Shaw, prepare to face the camera.

Left: P.W. Pemberton & Sons Ltd were musical instrument sellers and dealers. Their shop on Elliott Street, Tyldesley, flew the Union Jack and was gaily decorated for the 1913 royal visit of George V and Queen Mary.

Below: This clothiers and tailor's shop on Elliott Street, Tyldesley, run by the Ward brothers, was festooned with bunting and pictures of King George V and Queen Mary to celebrate a royal visit to the area on 12 July 1913.

Opposite above: Samuel Yates' blacksmith shop in the 1920s could be found in Market Street, Atherton, opposite the parish church. Here, a couple of workers are taking a break from their manual duties of shoeing and jobbing as they stand outside the smithy.

Below: Arthur Turtle, born in Tyldesley in 1888, was the manager of this grocery shop during the First World War. After refusing to join the army in 1916 as a conscientious objector, he was sent to prison for two-and-a-half years. Although originally a Methodist he later became a Quaker. An admirer of Gandhi and the writings of Tolstoy, Arthur was a keen vegetarian and opened one of the first health food shops in Leigh. He died at the Abacus Rest Home in Southport in December 1982.

Above: Richard Maxwell Stothert was the son of Richard Stothert the founder of Stotherts Ltd, manufacturing chemists of Atherton. The business was first established in 1852 at a little pharmacist shop in Bolton. When he was seventeen years old Richard joined his father, and after attending to correspondence early in the morning they spent the afternoons going to shops selling boxes of pills at a penny a box. By 1885 the business became known as Richard Stothert & Son, and in 1914 it was converted to a private limited company known as Stothert's Ltd. By 1949 the firm employed 450 employees. At his death in December 1948 at St Anne's on Sea, Richard was governing director of the firm, president of the Bolton Branch of the Commercial Traveller Association, a former governor of St Anne's Memorial Hospital and a member of the Tyldesley Lodge of Freemasons. In his will he left £321,132.

Opposite: Barrs, a soft drinks manufacturer which was established in 1935, took over the firm of Stothert's in 1967, with Mr R.H. Stothert remaining as Managing Director. For publicity purposes the company allowed a model to take a free ride on top of boxes being moved by a fork-lift truck.

Above: Working in the packaging department of Stothert's factory, *c.* 1920. Stothert's produced a wide range of products, from drinks to medicines.

Left: This typical grocery store, with its well-stocked shelves, was located in Elliott Street, Tyldesley, in the early 1960s and was owned by the Maypole Dairy Co.

The Savoy, a purpose-built cinema erected at the Punch Bowl, Atherton, was commissioned by the Eagle Picturedome Co. Ltd of Wigan. It was officially opened on 17 January 1927 by Mr C. Rowland JP, Chairman of Atherton District Council, who was presented with a golden key on behalf of Massey Bros of Pendleton, the builders. The first ever film to be shown was *The Sea Beast* starring John Barrymore and was shown on two consecutive nights. The cost of admission was balcony 10d; stalls 8d; pit 5d. The final week's programme in August 1967 featured *The Great St Trinians Train Robbery* starring Frankie Howard, and *Tobruk* with Rock Hudson and George Peppard. Following its closure the venue became a bingo hall before its present function as a snooker hall.

The interior view of a gentleman's outfitter shop belonging to Harry Fowles in Market Street, Atherton, during the early 1940s.

six

Education

On 5 July 1930, a party of twelve schoolgirls from Tyldesley Council School left for a month's trip to Hamburg, accompanied by four teachers. Also in the company were some German girls who had been staying in Tyldesley. Miss E.D. Brooks (headmistress) was in charge of the group. For those not travelling with the party, goodbyes were said at Tyldesley station.

In the mid-1930s these boys from the Hesketh Fletcher Church of England Senior School gymnastics team showed off their skills.

Above: Headmaster George Beddow, the central figure seated behind the globe, is seen here surrounded by his fellow teachers from Tyldesley Council schools in the early 1900s.

Right: George Beddow, a native of Pembrokeshire, was trained as a teacher at the Westminster Training College, London, before becoming the first headmaster of the Boothstown Wesleyan School after its opening on 18 August 1884. He remained in post eighteen years before accepting the headmastership of Tyldesley Upper George Street Council Schools. On his retirement in April 1926 after nearly forty-two years' service in the district, he was presented with a mahogany clock with Westminster chimes. For many years he had also been a part-time science teacher at Tyldesley Technical School. Mr Beddow, who died in January 1942, was a prominent member of Tyldesley chapel (Presbyterian) and frequently preached sermons and conducted services there.

During the miners strike in 1912, Chowbent School also became a soup kitchen, where children could be sure of a square meal, as seen in this early image.

Above: In the early 1950s, infant schoolchildren were frequently encouraged to take an afternoon nap in the classroom. Here, it is the turn of the pupils at Laburnum Street Church of England Infants School, Atherton.

Opposite below: An internal view of a classroom at Sacred Heart Primary School, Hindsford, taken in September 1996. This was the month when two separate sites consisting of the infant and junior departments came together.

Above: An aerial view of the Fred Longworth County Secondary School (now Fred Longworth High). It was officially opened on Saturday 7 March 1964 by Sir Herbert Andrew, KC, MG, CB, MA, who was permanent secretary to the Ministry of Education. It was built in eighteen months at a cost of £263,398. Initially the provision was for an intake of 420 girls which was to become a seven-form entry mixed school catering for 1,050 pupils. The first chairman of the school governors was county Alderman Fred Longworth, after whom the school was named. Miss A. Green was appointed as first headmistress. With changes in educational philosophy, the school became comprehensive in 1976 and by the 1990s had achieved arts college status. In the late 1990s its student intake had increased to 1,255 and by 2002 Ofsted inspectors reported that the school was amongst the top ten per cent in Britain. The headmaster responsible for helping staff achieve this high standard was Tony Colley.

During the nineteenth century, state-assisted elementary education was introduced in several stages, although attendance was not made compulsory until 1880. This photograph of children in a class at Chowbent British School, Bolton Road, Atherton, was taken in around 1895 and provides an unusual amount of detail illustrating conditions in a Victorian classroom. The pupils appear to be learning about the circulation of blood. The head teacher, standing beside the blackboard, is Isaiah Barker, who service as head of the school stretched from 1871 to 1914. After retirement he moved back to his native town of Kidderminster.

In 1960, teachers and pupils from a class at Tyldesley Central School pose for a class photograph.

The main school associated with St Anne's Mission church at Hindsford was opened in February 1876 by Mrs Lee of Alder House. It cost approximately £1,200 and had places for 350 boys. However, an additional infants' school was erected in February 1895 to accommodate a further 250 pupils. Children and teachers from a class of this new infants' school took a break from lessons in 1896 to sit for the photographer. The headmaster J.C. Carruthers, who had been appointed in 1876, remained in post for nearly forty-three years, retiring in 1921. He died at Bradford at the end of December 1924.

Seven-year-old Yvonne Dodger who was crowned Rose Queen of St George's Infants School, Atherton, in June 1978, is pictured with some of the pupils who took part in the festival at the school.

> *School wags for atherton Poor Children toll 29 of September 1747*
>
> | | | |
> |---|---|---|
> | Esther Smiths Child for reading 12 weeks - - - - | 0 · 1 · 0 |
> | Peter Kents Child for reading 5 weeks - - - - - | 0 · 0 · 5 |
> | Bostocks two Children for reading 4 weeks - - - | 0 · 0 · 2 |
> | James Smiths two Children for reading 8 weeks - - | 0 · 1 · 4 |
> | another Child of Bostocks for kniting & reading 12 weeks | 0 · 1 · 6 |
> | Thomas foddoth for reading 24 weeks - - - - - | 0 · 2 · 0 |
> | and for reading & sowing 12 weeks more - - - | 0 · 2 · 0 |
> | | 0 · 8 · 11 |
>
> Nov. 11. 1747 - Rec the Contents from Mr Brideoake
> accted for   by - John Hilton

A school fees account for Atherton schoolchildren was made out in 1747 by the Overseer of the Poor. The document indicates that children were given lessons in reading, sewing and knitting. The source of the educational establishment is not known, but a grammar school and a school associated with Chowbent chapel existed at the time.

Although there was an exhibition of aids for the physically handicapped and an open day at Fourways centre at Tyldesley on 27 September 1974, the official opening by Harold Wilson had to be postponed because of election plans. However Mr Wilson the Prime Minister did eventually open the centre, which caters for the needs of physically-handicapped school leavers, on Friday 14 March 1975. Wearing a tie clip with a wheelchair insignia, Mr Wilson was told that the object of Fourways was to enable the handicapped to become integrated into the community, and to lead as normal lives as possible. The capacity of the centre was thirty-five students, the first principal being Miss Kathleen Bruce.

seven

Atherton Photographic Society

F. PICKFORD ... ING FOR THE POOR
— HIMSEL... '39

Frank Pickford, a local businessman, had a keen interest in photography. After talking to a few friends and other interested parties he took the first steps in forming a local society by holding an inaugural meeting in the Atherton Church House on Thursday 7 April 1938. The main aims of such an organisation were to help and educate anyone interested in photography through mutual co-operation. From this meeting a fledgling society was formed, which became known as the Atherton and District Amateur Photographic Society. At the meeting the main officers were elected, these being Mr T. Lee Syms, President; Mr E.O. Staveley, Vice President; and Frank Pickford, Secretary. On 21 April 1938, a fortnight later, the first meeting proper took place, once again Church House being the venue. In 1939, with hat in hand, he jokingly attempts to raise money for the poor, particularly himself, abetted by a monkey.

Photographic society members posing for a group photograph during their outing to Borsdane Wood, Hindley, in 1940.

In 1972 a decision was made to extend the society's clubroom in order that indoor toilet facilities, a dark room, kitchen and a large working area could be added. Among members helping with the building work were Eric Dumble, Peter Hatch and Joan Szymanowski.

Members of the society prepare for one of their regular evening meetings in their clubroom ,in around 1950.

The first-ever group photograph of ADAPS members was taken on 5 May 1938 when they attended a working session at T. Lee Syms' studio in Tyldesley. The model for the evening was Edith Blears.

The first exhibition by members of the society from the clubhouse of the Wheatsheaf Hotel, Atherton, was held in a local school during the 1939/40 season. Those named in the picture were society members.

Atherton and District Amateur Photographic Society members at a meeting in the Wheatsheaf Hotel, Atherton, in the early 1950s.

Members of the photographic society meet in their new clubrooms at Back Stanley Street, Atherton, probably for the Atherton whole plate regional photographic competition in 1970.

Above: The annual photographic exhibition was held at Hesketh Fletcher School, probably in the late 1940s or early '50s. Besides the photographic prints on display, there was also a selection of equipment to look at.

Left: Seen here in around 1940 wearing naval uniform, John Burrows was a member of the society who was obviously enjoying being photographed with his Leica camera. In civilian life he was a bus driver with the Lancashire United Transport (L.U.T.). The photograph was probably taken whilst he was on active service during the Second World War.

Opposite above: In the 1950s, Reg Collier and Thornton Pickard led members in a club portrait evening.

Opposite below: In 1939 the society held a prize presentation evening at Lane Top School. Mr E.O. Staveley is seen presenting an award to Mr Frank Pickford.

Above: In the late 1950s an exhibition of members' photographs was held outside Hesketh Fletcher School in Market Street, Atherton.

Left: In July 1938 T. Lee Syms was in contemplative mood during the first outing of the society to Liverpool Docks. Syms was a well-known professional photographer who ran a photographic studio in Castle Street, Tyldesley. His credentials were impeccable, as he was an Honorary Fellow and past President of the Royal Photographic Society and also Vice President of the Lancashire and Cheshire Photographic Union. Unfortunately, although he was appointed the first President of Atherton Photographic Society in April 1938, he did not live to see it become affiliated to the Lancashire and Cheshire Photographic Union in January 1939, as he had died in the previous October. However, it was through his enthusiasm for the subject that he inspired others, which has helped to make it a thriving local society. It even has its own web site: www.adaps.idealnet.co.uk/history.htm

eight

Entertainment and Leisure

The central figure in the back row of this photograph from the 1930s is Mrs Leonard Fletcher who was Captain to this company of Girl Guides from the 1st Leigh, 1st Howe Bridge Brigade. Known to the girls as 'Mrs Leonard', she ensured that their outfits were both neat and of the best quality serge. Each girl paid 25s towards the cost of their uniform with Mrs Leonard contributing the rest of the money. She also bought two standards to be used on parade.

Right: The cast of
Tyldesley Amateur
Dramatics Society are
pictured here during their
dress rehearsal at Tyldesley
Little Theatre for their
production of *Darling Mr
London* in October 1980.

Below: Queen Alexandra,
Consort of King Edward
VII, was known for her
charity work. In 1912
she instituted the annual
Alexandra Rose Day
in aid of hospitals. This
Tyldesley group can be
seen posing beside their
decorated motor car in
the 1920s. The flower
days tended to be held at
the end of July and were
intended to raise money
for the Manchester and
Salford hospitals.

Opposite below: Visitors enjoying the flowers in the sunken garden at Atherton Park, 1949. Behind
the gardener on the left is the 'Monkey Shed'. The park was opened to the public in 1912.

The Red Lion Hotel on Church Street, Atherton, operated as a fully-licensed house belonging to Jos. Sharman & Sons, Mealhouse Lane, Bolton, on a lease from Lord Lilford estates in 1867. Walker Ales were supplied by George Shaw and Co Ltd. One of the earliest licensees in the 1820s and '30s was Henry Shepherd. Like many public houses it was the venue for meetings of friendly societies and in July 1869 the Duke of Sussex Lodge of Female Druids sat down to an anniversary dinner. During the mid-1880s it was the venue for music hall entertainment. Amongst those engaged to perform was Miss Hetty Eugenie, American song and dance artiste, sand, pump, skipping rope and champion lady slab dancer of the world!

Judges and officials at the annual show held at the Botanical Gardens, Cinder Hill, in September 1981 examine one of the prize-winning onions. Regular flower, fruit and vegetable shows had been held here since the Atherton and Tyldesley Botanical Association formally opened the gardens in September 1876. The association was established by the working men who were members of the United Botanical Association of Atherton and Tyldesley.

This mobile advertising campaign is promoting the Majestic Cinema, Tyldesley, in 1927. The vehicle can be seen parked outside the cinema in Castle Street. The building is now the swimming baths.

These participants in a mother and baby contest, which was held at the Alder House football ground, pose for the photographer in 1914.

For the Benefit of the SINGERS at the *New Chapel, Chowbent.*
On THURSDAY the 5th of JANUARY, 1786,
WILL BE PERFORMED,
At the Houſe of Mr. W I L L I A M   F I L D E S,
The Sign of the *King's-Head* in *Chowbent,*

A Grand Concert of vocal and inſtrumental

M U S I C,

Conſiſting of the following Pieces;
Aɛt the Firſt from *Samſon,* by G. F *Handel,* Eſq.

Overture.
Recit. This day a ſolemn feaſt, &c.
Chor. Awake the trumpet's lofty ſound.
Song. Then free from ſorrow
Song. Honour and arms.

Recit. Dagon ari , &c.
Song. To ſong and dance.
And Chorus, ditto.
Song. Let the bright ſeraphims.
Chor. Let their celeſtial concerts all unite

Aɛt the Second from JUDAS, by G. F. *Handel.*

Symphony by *Warnal,* with horns, &c.
Recit. I feel, &c.
Song. Arm, arm ye brave.
Chor. We come in bright array.
Recit. To heaven's Almighty King.
Air. Come ever ſmiling liberty.
Recit. O Judas, &c.
Air. 'Tis liberty alone.
Duet. Come ever ſmiling liberty.
Chor. Lead on, lead on, &c.
Recit. So will'd my father.

Chor. Diſdainful of danger.,
Duet & Chor. Hail, hail.
Song. Sound an alarm.
Chor. We hear, &c.
Recit. Enough, to heaven, &c.
Cho. of youths. See the conquering hero.
Cho. of vir. See the godlike youth, &c.
And full *chorus* after.
March & Duet. O lovely peace.
Song. Rejoice O Judah.
Chor. Hallelujah, &c.

Aɛt the Third from ACIS and GALATEA.

Overture.
Chor. O the pleaſures of the plains
Song & Chor. For us the zephyr blows.

Duet & Chor. Happy we, &c.
Song. Love founds th' alarm.
Trio. The flocks ſhall leave,&c.

To conclude with *HANDEL's* CORONATION ANTHEM.

The Principal Performers from *Wigan, Hindley, Aſhton, Bolton, Chowbent,* &c.
The Choruſſes to be as full as poſſible, with Kettle-Drums, Trumpets, Violincellos, &c.
The Drums by Maſter *Entwiſle,* Organiſt, at *Wigan.*

The Whole conduɛted by Mr. *Thomas Entwiſle* of *Wigan.*

Tickets at 1s. 6d. each to be had of Mr. *Peter Valentine,* Mr. *Richard Worthington,*
Doɛtor *Crook, Chowbent,* Doɛtor *Gueſt, Leigh,* and Mr. *Peter Arrowſmith of Aſtley.*
The Concert to begin at Six o'Clock in the evening. After the Concert there will
be an Aſſembly, for ſuch Ladies and Gentlemen as purchaſe Tickets. Muſic *gratis*

Above: Taken during the late Victorian period, these Athertonians can be seen sitting outside the house in their front garden taking part in the ritual of drinking afternoon tea.

Left: One of the earliest performances of Handel's music in the area occurred in January 1786 at the King's Head, Atherton. Excerpts from some of his most popular works were performed, with musicians coming from the surrounding area. The conductor was Thomas Entwistle of Wigan who was the organist at Wigan parish church. At one time he had been with the company of Kena's Strolling Players. He was married to a Mrs Mellon, whose daughter Harriot was later to become a famous actress. She had married Thomas Coutts in 1815, then after his death married the Duke of St Albans, thus attaining the title Duchess of St Albans. Tradition has it that Handel stayed at Bedford House, the home of Mr Guest in 1742, and played the organ there.

Above: Atherton public brass bandsmen regaled in boater hats pose for the photographer in 1910 after winning first prize in a brass band contest. The first Atherton brass band contest was held in August 1895 when the first prize to be awarded was £30 and a sheep.

Right: With the advent of rock 'n' roll in the late 1950s and an ever growing market for teenage popular music, many local record shops began to cater specifically for this particular group of consumers. Besides enabling people to listen to music before purchasing their records (singles, EP's or LP's) in sound-proof booths, local retailers such as Harold Smith of Tyldesley began to advertise their top selling records in local newspapers. This listing is from the *Leigh Journal* of November 1961.

Above: On 1 January 1902 the Coffee Pot was officially opened by Mr Miles Burrows to be run as a temperance public house. Opening times were the same as those of an ordinary licensed house, including Sundays. The building comprised various sized rooms, the largest being the main coffee room measuring 32ft by 16ft. Facilities were used by the YMCA. In the 1930s a men's service club was established to give work miners and ex-servicemen the opportunity to learn new skills. The Coffee Pot also served as a venue for inquests. An advertisement for cheap meals in 1911 gave the following prices: steak puddings 3d, potatoes 1d, vegetables 1d and milk pudding 1d.

Opposite below: Although born in Leigh in June 1965, British chess player Nigel Short spent his early years in Atherton. He was educated at Bolton School and Leigh College, and by the age of twelve had beaten Jonathan Penrose in the British Championship. However, an early success was against one of the Soviet grandmasters, Victor Korchnoi. Here he is playing Korchnoi in the *Evening Standard* London Championship of 1976, where he won game fifteen with his black pieces. Nigel was to become Grand Master in 1984, British Champion in 1984 and 1987 and English Champion in 1991. By 1993 he had defeated Anatoly Karpov and Garri Kasparov. After resigning from the World Chess Federation he set up the Professional Chess Association with Kasparov in 1993. In 1999 he was awarded an Honorary MBE; ranked seventh in the world. He is now chess columnist for the *Sunday Telegraph*.

Above: May 1977 was the beginning of a series of annual festivals held in Tyldesley. In 1982, after seven years of pram racing the prams were replaced by wheelbarrows and wellies. There was a mixed turnout for this fancy-dress race through the town centre. First over the line were three soccer players, Jim Colloby, Vic Crompton and Stuart Crilly.

Left above: Tyldesley Allotments and Smallholders Club held their annual show on Saturday 29 August 1981, when fifty-two entrants had over 400 exhibits. The National Allotments blue ribbon and certificate of merit, as well as the Dahlia Society's silver medal went to R. Everett whilst Dennis Holmes won the T.E. Gilman Cup for the tenant members. Amongst other winners was R. Smith who received the National Society of Leisure Gardeners' plaque for the best exhibit.

One of the most interesting features of the Tyldesley Wakes of September 1925 was the bullock roasting, a custom revived after an absence of thirty-three years by Billy Mitchell and others. At eight o'clock in the morning, a bullock weighing twenty-eight stone, was chained to a revolving spit, with a cartwheel at one end. The wheel was turned continually until night time on the instruction of Fred Taylor of Stratford-upon-Avon, the self-styled world champion ox roaster. At two o' clock in the afternoon the first slice was cut by Tyldesley's oldest inhabitant, ninety-three-year-old James Owen. About one hundred four-pound loaves were purchased to enable sandwiches to be made, and these were sold at sixpence each. Over 2,000 were sold and by eight o' clock the carcass had been stripped clean.

Mary or Marie Fuller (stage name 'Santoi') was born into a show business family. Her mother Marie, a well-known performer, had appeared in various light musical shows and at the peak of her career could command a fee of £600 per week. She died in Bradford Royal Infirmary in July 1924 after performing on stage and her body was brought back to Tyldesley cemetery for burial. Her daughter Mary, a comedienne in her own right, had three sisters and one brother. One sister, Jose, became a famous soubrette, another married into the fairground business, and the last, Honor Margaret Rozelle Santoi Fuller, was to become a well-known actress under the stage name 'Jill Summers' who immortalised the character Phyllis Pearce in *Coronation Street*. Her brother was Tom F. Moss, a vocalist. In the early years Tom and Jill appeared as a double act during their tour of the halls.

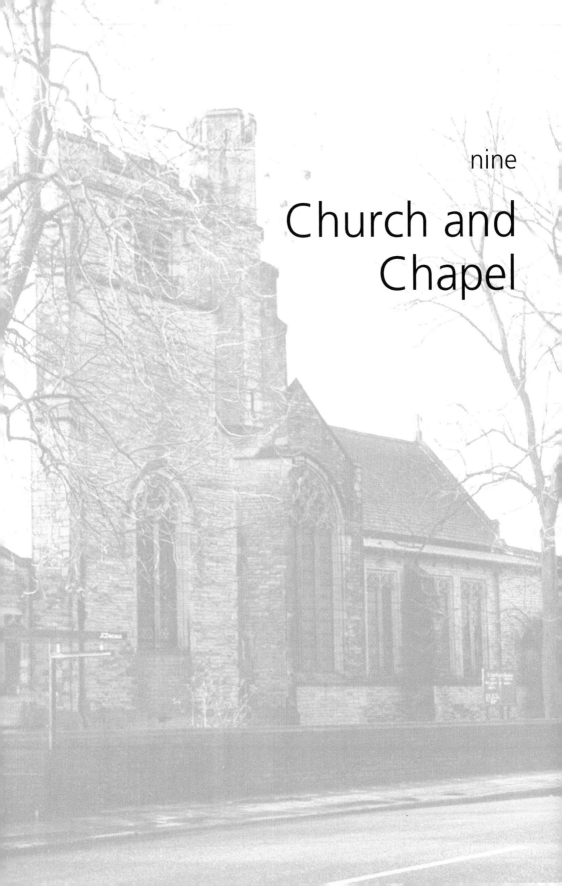

nine

Church and
Chapel

The Mission Hall at Atherton was situated at the corner of Alma Street and Mealhouse Lane. Founded by James Rawlinson in 1876, the hall was built brick by brick by his enthusiastic followers. It was officially opened for services on Good Friday in 1877 and welcomed people until October 1968 when it was demolished. This photograph was taken just before the building disappeared. Originally Mr Rawlinson held religious meetings in a warehouse in the Market Place but as his followers increased he had to find larger premises. Because no one was ever turned away from the mission and ragged children were cared for, it became fondly known as the Mission and Ragged School. After his death in 1905, the work of the mission was continued by his dear wife and her friend Mrs G.M. Fawell.

On 1 May 1948 this group photograph was taken after the induction of the Revd H.D. Rosenthall as Vicar of St John the Baptist, Atherton. The new vicar is on the left with the Archdeacon of Manchester Revd A. Selwyn Bean centre, and the Rural Dean of Leigh, Revd C.K.K. Prosser on the right. Behind are churchwardens, Messrs J. Ackers and H.E. Hayes. Before arriving in Atherton, Mr Rosenthall had seen service in the Far East – including New Zealand, Singapore and Hong Kong.

Welsh Baptists had been meeting in Tyldesley since the 1870s. Various venues were used as meeting places, until January 1894 when their own chapel was opened for worship. Situated at the corner of Milk Street and Shuttle Street, the building cost £580. Like all chapels, they had their own male voice choir whose members can be seen here.

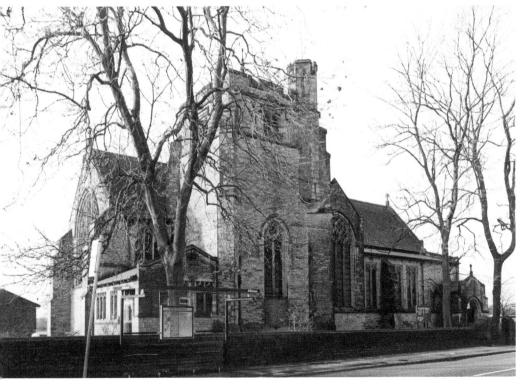

A view of St Anne's, Hindsford, in January 1999. Hindsford was constituted as an independent parish on 26 June 1884 before the present building was consecrated on 31 January 1901 by Bishop Moorhouse of Manchester. Worshippers had frequented a similar mission church on Swan Island, which had become too small for its original purpose. Unfortunately, the building has now closed and is no longer used for services because of structural problems and dry rot.

The Sacred Heart church at Hindsford as it looked in September 1996. The foundation stone for the church was laid by the Right Revd Dr Goss, Lord Bishop of Liverpool in June 1868. Land for this purpose had been given by Lord Lilford. Designed in the early English style by Edward Kirby of Liverpool, its nave measurements were approximately 72ft by 37ft and there was accommodation for about 500 worshippers. Father Richard O'Neill was appointed the First Parish Priest. The same architect was responsible for a wall around the church, which was laid in 1875. By 2002 this Grade II listed building was under the threat of closure because of the falling number of worshippers.

This view of Atherton parish church was taken in February 1948 from Tyldesley Road (previously known as Dan Lane). The church, which stands on the site of two former churches, dates back to the seventeenth century. It was built at the instigation of Ralph Fletcher Junior in two main stages, the architects being Paley and Austin of Lancaster. In 1991 the building was subject to an arson attack but has since been rebuilt. The turreted building on the left initially belonged to William Deacon Bank. Opened in 1893 it was designed by Bradshaw and Gass of Bolton in the Renaissance style, three stories high using Edwards red brick and terracotta.

Above: Tyldesley parish church, photographed in 1984, is dedicated to St George the Martyr, was consecrated on 19 September 1825 by Charles James Blomfield, Bishop of Chester. The design was by Sir Robert Smirke RA in the Gothic style. Smirke was a well-known architect who was elected to the Royal Academy in 1811 holding the position of Treasurer there from 1820-1850. Amongst the buildings he designed were those of the Covent Garden Theatre, The Royal Mint at Tower Hill, The British Museum and the Royal College of Physicians. The first minister of the church was Jacob Robson who held office there until his death in 1851. One interesting burial in the churchyard was that of Richard Halliwell (a dentist) who died in July 1859. In his will it requested that all the teeth he had extracted be buried with him. This amounted to 30,000 in number and they weighed 64lbs.

Right: In June 1978 these children from St George's church in Atherton helped to keep the banner upright when they took part in the annual Procession of Witness.

The Salvation Army was founded by William Booth in 1865 and it was called The Christian Revival Association. By 1878 it had received its present form and title, being organised on military lines. There was certainly an active group based in Atherton by 1881 when the army consisted of five men, two women and two children. Music has always been associated with the Salvation Army and in 1959 this group photograph was taken of members and their musical instruments.

On 5 August 1978, Valerie Aldred aged twelve was crowned Bag Lane Methodist church Rose Queen by Mrs Farnworth. Valerie's sister Marion had been the first queen in 1976, whilst the retiring queen was Angela Rose. The crown bearer was Scott Williams and the train bearers included Heather Pollard, Caren and Adele Williams, Allison Banks and Tania Freeborn.

Junior choristers from St Michael and All Angel's church at Howebridge, sitting in their robes outside the vestry door at the back of the church. The occasion was the celebration of Queen Victoria's Diamond Jubilee. The vicar on the right is the Revd William Robert Clayton, whilst the lady on the left is probably his wife. Four members of the choir have been identified: George Thorpe (first left, back row), Thomas Battersby (third from left, back row), John Heyes (second from left, middle row) and finally Sam Hughes (fifth from left, middle row). In the following year Sam Hughes received a book prize entitled *Britain's Roll of Glory, the Victoria Cross* for regular attendance and good conduct in the choir.

A 1908 postcard from Tyldesley Top chapel. The Revd Donald Jarvis was minister here from 1907 until 1915, when he tendered his resignation in order to take up a similar position in the city of Bath. He intended to preach at the same chapel that George Whitfield had preached in and live in the same house where Selina, Countess of Huntingdon had lived. The Countess of Huntingdon – having been influenced by Wesleyan Methodism – set about erecting chapels in different parts of the land. One of these was in Tyldesley itself in 1798, where it was locally known as the Lady Huntingdon chapel.

Above: In the early 1900s members of the Irish National Foresters gathered outside the Sacred Heart church at Hindsford. The Irish National Foresters were originally a branch of the British-based Ancient Order of Foresters, a friendly society, but by the late 1870s had seceded from it and adopted a strong nationalist tone with a distinctive Irish history. It was later to become the largest Irish Friendly Society.

Opposite above: Tyldesley Wesleyan chapel, which was opened by the Revd Dr Young in 1887 and was located in Lower Elliott Street, has now been demolished. This internal view, which was taken by local photographer Thomas Lee Syms JP in about 1920 suggests a strong Anglican influence with its altar rail, raised pulpit and organ.

Opposite below left: Stained-glass windows are one of many distinguishing features of church architecture. This particular memorial window dedicated to Mr and Mrs Abraham Burrows was installed in the new Atherton Baptist church when it opened for worship on 1 July 1903. The building was subsequently demolished in the mid-1980s and rebuilt on the same site. The stained-glass window was transferred into the new place of worship.

Opposite below right: This early nineteenth-century postcard shows both the spiritual and secular side of the Tyldesley township. However, in appearance it suggests that the earthly delights are certainly more appealing than the religious ones!

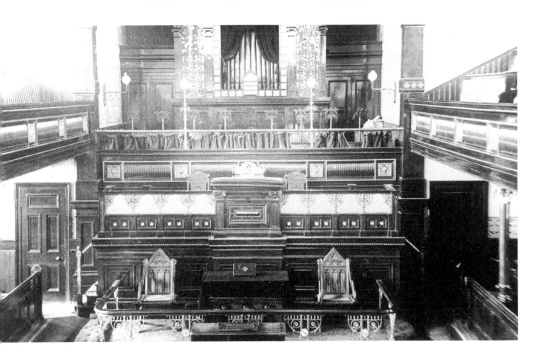

THE WESLEYAN CHAPEL.

The people here in Tyldesley are
so hospitable, that there is hardly
anything they wont do, to ensure
one having a good time.

One unusual feature of Chowbent chapel is this oak-built three-decker pulpit. The oak for the pulpit and for many of the pews was grown locally in Squire Hulton's Park. The word 'pulpit' comes from the Latin *pulpitum*, meaning a raised place for reading during mealtimes – commonly found in monasteries. However it is now seen as a place from which members of a congregation are preached to. Three-decked pulpits were common during the eighteenth century, with the first tier being used as a clerk's desk, the middle one as a lectern and the topmost tier as a pulpit.

Tyldesley cemetery, which was opened in 1878, contained three chapels. This one, photographed in October 1984, has since been demolished.

The Revd Thomas Jackson-Smith (formerly Thomas Jackson Smith) was educated at the University of London, St Bees and University College of Durham. The Church of England ministers took him to Northwood, Staffordshire, and St Michael of All Angels Atherton 1871/72 before becoming incumbent at St Peters, Queenstown, New Zealand for the period 1872-1875. On his return to England he took up a position as perpetual curate, first in the museum church and then in its rebuilt church of St Michael and All Angels at Howe Bridge. He remained here until 1879 before becoming Vicar of St Thomas at Bedford, Leigh. He retired from the ministry in 1909 after which he lived in Bournemouth before his death in 1917.

Four ministers of the Chowbent chapel.

Top left: Revd Harry Toulmin (1766-1823) was the eldest son of Joshua Toulmin DD, dissenting historian and biographer. Born at Taunton and having attended the Hoxton Academy, he became minister at Monton before moving to Chowbent. He was minister here from 1788-1792 after which he emigrated to America where he became successively President of the Transylvania College of Lexington, Kentucky; Secretary to the state of Kentucky; Judge of the Mississippi territory and then a member of the State Assembly of Alabama.

Top right: Revd Benjamin Rigby Davies (1770-1835), a native of Wigston, Leicestershire succeeded Toulmin in 1793. He officiated at Chowbent for a period of forty-three years.

Below left: Revd John Harrison MA, PhD (1815-1866) was minister at the chapel between 1838 and 1847, after which he moved to Ipswich. His father was an able mathematician, linguist and musician.

Below right: Revd Marmaduke Charles Frankland (1815-1888) was born in Leeds. He was the oldest son of John Frankland, a large cloth manufacturer. He was educated at Leeds Grammar School, then Manchester New College, York. His first ministry was at Malton in Yorkshire, then Whitby before moving to Atherton in 1852. He lived at the Laburnums and was interested in the free library movement, education and temperance as well being a member of the Atherton Burial Board.

ten

Sport

The second annual sports day organised by the welfare society associated with Howe Bridge Spinning Company's Mills took place at the end of August 1919. There were both men and women's tug-of-war competitions on the day, the men's section being won by the Engineer's Department, ('Nobbie's Gang'). Prizes to the winners were presented by Colonel Fletcher JP.

In 1964 Edmund Norris and his father Fred were seen running together in a ten-mile race at Massachusetts. Fred Norris, a Tyldesley long-distance runner, twice represented Great Britain in the Olympic Games before he emigrated to America in the early 1960s. In 1952 he was entered in the 10,000 metres at Helsinki where he was placed eighth. Four years later he attempted the marathon but did not finish the race, which was held in Melbourne. However, he was honoured in Tyldesley where the council presented him with a gold wristwatch from a testimonial fund which had been opened for him. Fred – who is now in his seventies and still running for the love of it – is a great ambassador for the sport and one of Britain's most distinguished distance runners of the post-war era.

Although plans for this sports centre originated with the old Atherton Council in November 1963, it managed to survive the threat of the axe after local government reorganisation and was officially opened on 3 March 1977 by the Duchess of Gloucester. Also in attendance were Mayor Councillor Albert Eckersley and Councillor Len Sumner who was Chairman of the Recreation Committee. The complex, which was built at Howebridge on the site of six old pit shafts, cost £1.4m. The first manager of the centre was John Carr.

In 1908 Tyldesley Swimming Club's senior water polo team became the Manchester and District Champions.

Some of the competitors at the George and Dragon are seen here as they prepare for a play-off in the National Ladies Pairs Darts, in August 1981.

Opposite above: On 30 April 1921 Mr A.E. Holt JP officially opened the tennis courts which were situated at the sports ground owned by Howe Bridge Spinning Mills on Flapper Fold Lane. Noticeable in the background are two gasometers belonging to Atherton Gas Company. The gas works were built in 1836 and demolished in 1961.

Opposite below left: In December 1932 William Mather, a sixteen-year-old from Hindsford who had attended St Anne's School was an apprentice jockey in Chantilly, France. He had returned home for a short holiday when this photograph was taken. He was working in the stables owned by Jack Cannington at Villa-des-Bois, where fifteen employees looked after fifty-two horses.

Opposite below right: By 1936 William Mather was a professional jockey. In June of the same year he won a French classic, the Prix de Sweepstake de Grand Prix de Paris. Riding Orachalque he took the first prize of 100,000 francs. On 2 October 1936, the *Leigh Chronicle* reported that twenty-one-year-old William had died in the hospital at Maisons Laffitte following serious injuries sustained as a result of an accident on the racecourse at Longchamps. His horse, Muscadet, running in the Prix du Ranelagh, was brought down by another horse ridden by A. Tucker. The French press had hailed him as a jockey with a fine future.

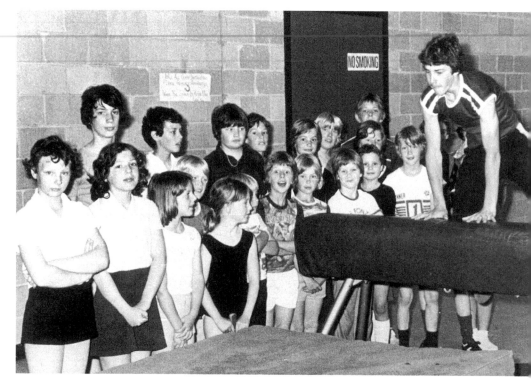

During the school holidays of July 1979, these youngsters at Howebridge sports centre watch fifteen-year-old Brian Rhodes as he uses the vaulting horse.

During the early 1950s the aim of the managerial committee of Briarcroft Boys' Club was to offer facilities for further education and recreation to boys of school-leaving age, and then for the first few years of their working life. Activities included arts and crafts, puppetry, dramatics, boxing and physical training. Here a group are trying their hand at wrestling.

In September 1923, this group of swimmers from the Atherton Club became Lancashire Junior Champions.

Annual swimming gala organised by the Tyldesley Swimming and Water Polo Club in around 1880. Caleb Wright JP, who first conceived the idea of providing public swimming baths for the people of Tyldesley, officially opened the facilities on 22 July 1876. The Tyldesley Swimming Club was officially formed at a meeting on 22 August 1876 when Mr Hadfield was appointed Secretary and Mr Clegg, Treasurer. At a later meeting Dr Duncan was elected first President and a membership subscription of five shillings was set. 15 September 1877 saw the first annual swimming gala of the club, which is still going from strength to strength.

Chowbent Races, 1775.

〰〰〰〰〰〰〰〰〰〰〰〰〰〰〰〰〰〰〰〰〰〰〰〰〰〰〰〰〰〰〰

To be RUN for, in the PARKS, near *Chowbent*,

On *Wednefday* the 26th of *July*, the *Gentlemen's Purfe*, Value 50l.

BY any Horfe, Mare, or Gelding, that never won above the Value of 40l. at any one Time, Matches excepted. Five Year olds to carry 8ft. 5lb. fix Year-olds 9ft. and Aged 9ft. 6lb. A Winner of one Prize, in the prefent Year, to carry 3lb. extraordinary, the Beft of three Four-mile Heats.———Entrance 5s. The Stakes to go to the fecond Beft.

On *Thurfday* the 27th will be Run for, the *Ladies Purfe*, Value 50l.

BY any Horfe, Mare, or Gelding, that never won above the Value of 30l. at any one Time, Matches excepted.———Entrance 4s. The Stakes to go to the fecond Beft, three Four-mile Heats.

On *Friday* the 28th will be Run for, the *Town's Subfcription*, Value 50l. *Give* and *Take.*

BY any Horfe, Mare, or Gelding, that never won above the Value of 40l. at any one Time, Matches excepted. Fourteen Hands, Aged, to carry 8ft. 7lb. higher or lower in Proportion, allowing 7lb. for every Year under feven. A Winner of one Prize, in the prefent Year, to carry 3lb. extraordinary, the Beft of three Four-mile Heats. To be fubject to the King's Plate Articles, and to fuch other Articles as will be then and there produced.

To enter and meafure at Mr. RICHARD ALDRED's BARN, two Days before Running, and to ftart each Day precifely at Three o'Clock. Three reputed Running Horfes to ftart each Day or no Race, unlefs agreed to by the Stewards.

N. B. No Perfon will be permitted to erect any Booth, or Stall, or to fell any Kind of Liquors or Victuals, but who fhall be Subfcribers to the faid Races.

☞ ORDINARIES and ASSEMBLIES as ufual.

One method of promoting sporting events before the advent of television and local newspapers was through the handbill. In 1775, Chowbent races were advertised in this fashion, the venue for this occasion probably being the grounds of Atherton Hall.

Opposite above: In October 1931 Tyldesley Rugby Union players pose for this team photograph. Amongst the group is W.E. Dowling, a popular player who had completed six seasons as captain in the April of that year. Dowling was educated at St Bees, Cumberland, before joining the team in 1919. Besides rugby, he was a keen sportsman, involved with football, boxing and wrestling. In 1918 he won the welter-weight boxing championship of the Air Force, whilst stationed at Bristol. Furthermore he was a member of the English wrestling team which took part in the 1924 Olympic Games in Paris where he was in the welter-weight class.

These Atherton ladies were members of a local bowling team who used the facilities at Central Park, Hamilton Street. They were captured on camera, probably in the late 1940s. One of the male visitors to this female gallery was Councillor S. Loveless. The earliest women's bowling handicap at Atherton took place in August 1935.

Above: Playing hockey on the field belonging to Howe Bridge Spinning Mills. Sometime around 1918 these four girls were taking time off work to improve their skills at the game on Flapper's Fold recreation ground.

Right: Ladies from Tyldesley Top chapel enjoy a game of croquet in the early 1920s.

Opposite above: Members of the Tyldesley Park bowling team which won the Lancashire County championship in September 1942. In the centre is Councillor B. Lee, chairman of the Tyldesley War Comforts Committee. In order to raise funds for the war effort, two matches were arranged against Bispham Hall. The second match was played on Tyldesley Park green where Tyldesley won by 87 points after losing the first by 20. Members of the team included:
R. Corrigan (Junior), J.W. Cartwright,
N. Warburton, R. Corrigan (Senior), W. Potter,
Ed Parsons, J. Bradbury, J.S. Howcroft,
N. Unsworth, H. Hughes, W. Davenport and C. Smith.

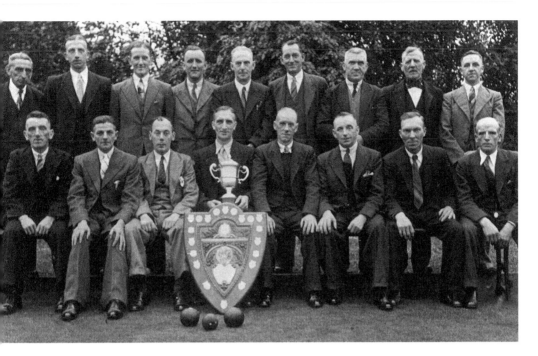

On 24 February 1923 a football team from Atherton Collieries beat Barnoldswich Town 4-1 to take the Lancashire Junior Shield. The match was played at Burnden Park and at the close of the game the shield was presented to Pedley. The collieries team consisted of Brown, Donough, Ford, T. Virgo, W. Pedley, V. Monaghan, W. May, T. Hook, A. Harris, H. Butler and W. Roberts.

Pigeon racing was a common feature of Northern life in the period before the First World War. In 1912 there were a number of local groups involved with this sport, including members of the Tyldesley and District Homing Society, some of whom can be seen in the photograph. During 1912 there was a Guernsey race as well as Stafford, Kidderminster, Worcester and Bournemouth one's. For the Guernsey race in June, eighteen Tyldesley members competed with 133 birds. Some of the competitors included J. Tipton, F. Clare, J.H. Makin, R. Croft and R. Higson.

Opposite: A few members of the Tyldesley Anglers Association who in September 1979 helped to raise funds to purchase a coach for their fishing trips. The club was formed in 1890 with headquarters at the George and Dragon. The longest standing member in 1979 was Mr Bert Pendlebury of Sussex Place who had joined the club on 8 September 1929.

Addin Tyldesley, son of Councillor Ralph Tyldesley who became clerk to Rothwell Urban Council was a local swimmer of repute who competed in the Olympic Games of 1908 when they were held in London. He swam in the 100 metres freestyle, clocking up a time of 1 minute 12 seconds. Unfortunately this was not good enough to win a medal, the gold being taken by Charles Daniels of the United States of America. Addin can be seen here standing in front of some of his trophies.

Left: Duncan Cleworth of Tyldesley was an international swimmer from the Tyldesley Swimming and Water Polo Club. In 1978 he represented England in the 4 x 100 metres individual medley at the Olympic Games and the 4 x 50 metres individual medley at the Commonwealth Games in Canada.

Below: Members of a Tyldesley billiards team with their cues in 1934. It is possible that they were the senior section of the Tyldesley chapel B team who were members of the institute's billiards league.

Above left: John 'Buff' Berry, a famous rugby player of the late Victorian era was born at Fellside near Kendal in 1866. He first rose to prominence after joining the famous Kendal Hornets, and later became a leading player in the early years of the Westmorland county club. In January 1888 he caused a sensation by moving to Tyldesley where he joined the local club. Within a few months he had so inspired his new club that they were victorious in the West Lancashire Cup. Under the influence of Berry, Tyldesley were to become one of the strongest sides in the country, earning the nickname of 'The Mighty Bongers'. By 1895 Tyldesley were to lift the Lancashire Club Championship, the same year which saw an irreparable split in the rugby structure with the formation of the Northern Union. Berry's long career, which ended in 1901, coincided with Tyldesley's demise. He died in May 1930 at the Manchester Royal Infirmary aged sixty-three.

Above right: Tyldesley Cricket Club was formed in the autumn of 1876 by Mr W.W. Walker, headmaster of St Anne's School, Hindsford. The original ground was close to St Anne's Mission church at the Chanters where it remained for three years before transferring to Shakerley, close to the toll bar. However, the ground was too small and ill-adapted for cricket, so the club moved once again, this time to Astley Street. The dressing room accommodation was inadequate and money was raised through subscription, initiated by the president Mr C. Eckersley for a new pavilion. The pavilion, which was officially opened in 1893, had been built in 1892 for the 'Old American' exhibition at Old Trafford by Neild & Son of Manchester and cost over £300. It was designed to serve the purposes of a cricket or a tennis club. It measured 22ft by 18ft and was about 34ft high and built of timber, with the outside frame consisting of twelve pitch-pine uprights 20ft long, standing on blocks of slag to which they were securely clamped. The ground floor consisted of a dressing room and lounge as did the upper storey where the lounge could accommodate fifty spectators. The sum paid for the pavilion was £109 but further expenses were incurred in its removing, rebuilding and alteration. This photograph of club members was taken in the early 1900s.

These five young ladies in costume could be seen at the Atherton Carnival and Gala held in May 1924, which was organised by the Atherton Collieries Joint Association. The event took place in the grounds of Alder House. Here the May Queen was crowned and spectators could also watch morris and maypole dancing as well as listen to jazz bands. A play entitled *Maypole Morning* was performed by the Atherton Collieries Joint Association Dramatic Society.

Acknowledgements

The author is grateful to Joan Szymanowski for producing information from the Howe Bridge church archives; John Charlson, Mrs H. Chadwick, James Chillingworth, Mrs J. Gallimore, the Atherton Photographic Society archives and others who have loaned photographs to the collection

Very special thanks are due to Len Hudson ARPS of Wigan Heritage Service for his valued assistance in photographic identification and reproduction, and to Stephanie Tsang and Amanda Bradshaw for undertaking the typing.

'Bent' and 'Bongs' are the local names for the two adjoining townships of Atherton and Tyldesley situated on the eastern side of Wigan Borough. Like similar small communities, which have been incorporated into a wider municipal area, they are still keen to defend their own individual identities. Their history is recorded through this compilation of over 200 archival photographs which cover a period from the mid-nineteenth century through to the present day when mills and mines once dominated the industrial landscape, but whose edifices are now but a memory for many. Hopefully the illustrations will provide a nostalgic trip into the past for the older generation who will remember trams and trolleybuses, of taking an afternoon nap in school, or even seeing a film at a local cinema, whilst providing an eye-opener to a younger age group who have never experienced such pleasures. Although Wigan Heritage Service – now a department within the newly-formed Wigan Leisure and Culture Trust – has supplied the majority of photographs for this publication, a small number have been lent by private individuals.